BRAIN-TWISTERS

1. Three boxes are labeled "Apples," "Oranges," and "Apples and Oranges." Each label is incorrect. You may select only one fruit from one box. How can you label each box correctly?

2. Punctuate the following so it makes sense: John while James had had had had had had had had had had a better effect on the teacher.

3. A snail is at the bottom of a well thirty feet deep. It can crawl upward three feet in one day, but at night it slips back two feet. How long does it take the snail to crawl out of the well?

4. "A rolling stone gathers no moss" means:
   (a) None of the Rolling Stones smoke marijuana.
   (b) Shifting stones around in a rock garden prevents weeds.
   (c) Rock collections don't appreciate in value with time.
   (d) Stay in your groove to do your thing.

Books by
James F. Fixx

Games For The Superintelligent
More Games For The Superintelligent
Solve It!

Published by
WARNER BOOKS

Games for the Super-intelligent

By James F. Fixx

WARNER BOOKS

A Warner Communications Company

For my father,
who started me wondering

WARNER BOOKS EDITION

Copyright © 1972 by James F. Fixx
All rights reserved.
Portions of this book originally appeared in *Playboy* Magazine.
Copyright © 1972 by Playboy Enterprises, Inc.
Published by arrangement with Doubleday & Company.

Warner Books, Inc.
666 Fifth Avenue
New York, N.Y. 10103

W A Warner Communications Company

Printed in the United States of America

First Warner Books Printing: December, 1982

10 9 8 7

Confessions of
a thoroughly puzzled man

For as long as I can remember I have taken a special
—some might say an almost irrational—delight in
puzzles, games, and problems of all sorts. At one time
I devised, or at least tried to devise, formulas for some
wondrously worthless calculations—for predicting
with what frequency an automobile odometer would
show a symmetrical number, such as 00100 or 50505
or 99999, for finding the sum of a string of consecutive
numbers, for computing the interrelationship of speed,
spin, direction, and depth of a crosscourt backhand
(that one, somehow, never worked out very well).
And I can still remember how I felt, while taking a
college physics course, when the professor wrote on
the blackboard a formidably complicated formula
that turned out, as soon as one understood it, to be
absolutely startling in its elegance and simplicity. I

knew, at that moment, that I was looking on beauty bare.

The feeling I experienced at that time, though I can no longer even remember what the formula was, has never left me. I am still awed and fascinated by any really good mathematical morsel, and I confess to such indefensible aberrations as having once ridden a train far past my stop while trying to figure out why a dozen or so apparently quite practical perpetual motion machines described in *Scientific American* wouldn't work. (Curse you, Gerard Piel!) This, then, is the book of a thoroughly committed man, a True Believer when it comes to a certain variety of mental shenanigans.

What, exactly, is that variety? Well, as will be seen, the puzzles in this book all require little or no real expertise. Some of them look forbiddingly intricate, but you have my word that none of them really are that way. You don't need to be a nuclear physicist to solve any of them, and it is very likely, in fact, that if you happen to *be* a nuclear physicist, some of the puzzles will prove more troublesome than if you were less heavily burdened with mathematical sophistication.

No, what these puzzles all have is a kind of do-it-with-mirrors difficulty, a difficulty much more spurious than actual. And that's precisely what makes them the charming diversions they are. They all require some logical (or, on occasion, illogical) leap that, in human terms, is the rough equivalent of a monkey in a cage suddenly realizing that it needs to use a stick to reach a banana. No stick, no banana. And so it is here: No leap, no solution. If that seems obscure now, it won't take you long to see what is meant.

A book like this would have been all but impossible to compile and write had I not by chance stumbled onto a sort of mother lode of puzzles and puzzlers: an organization called Mensa, which has recruited its entire membership from the most intelligent 2 per cent of the population. Several years ago, upon first attending a Mensa meeting in order to write a magazine article about the group, I was startled when at meeting's end several M's, as they call themselves, got together over beer and pretzels not to tell bawdy stories or any other such thing but—*mirabile dictu!*—to swap puzzles with each other. It did not, however, occur to me until much later that there might be the makings of a book in the puzzle phenomenon. When it finally did, Mensa members—who are, among other things, the most certifiably superintelligent group in existence today—were of incalculable assistance. To solicit their help was to open a floodgate that kept me busily reading letters and, in more cases than one, scratching my head in happy puzzlement over their suggestions for many, many months. (The names of some of those from whom I have shamelessly stolen ideas appear at the end of this book.)

Lest I be charged with a singlemindedness I do not even begin to possess, I should perhaps mention that puzzling is far from the only thing I do, nor is it even *most* of what I do. And that's undoubtedly just as well, to judge by the look of glazed stupefaction that occa-

7

sionally creeps over the faces of people whose patience and kindly pretense are beginning to fray. (To some people, it seems, too many puzzles are like too many home movies.) No, puzzles are something the aficionado does in odd, wonderful moments, mostly alone, and he is very lucky indeed when on occasion he finds himself with an equally devoted partner-in-puzzles. Since there aren't many of us—compared, say, to hockey or baseball fans—it doesn't happen often.

So a very special welcome.

JAMES F. FIXX

Riverside, Connecticut
September 1971

Contents

I.

The pleasures of intelligence—
and some incidental perils

Practically all of us, whether we're bright or dull, tend to take it for granted that intelligence is a Good Thing and a lack of intelligence a Bad Thing—period. A little reflection will show, however, that it's not nearly that simple. Though very bright people seldom receive much sympathy for their brightness—a little incidental derision maybe, but not sympathy—they suffer along under handicaps undreamed of by their less gifted brethren. Nor are these, as one might suppose, simply the burdens imposed by a heightened awareness, a greater sense of life's complexities, a more poetic and sensitively tuned soul, etc., etc., etc. They are, on the contrary, provably distressing in quite practical ways—ways that bedevil virtually all those whose I.Q.s have never learned to play possum.

The problems of the superintelligent take a number of forms, but whatever they are they almost always start early. The following conversation, between a second-grade teacher and a bright pupil, is a cogently chilling case in point:

TEACHER: I am going to read you a series of numbers: 1, 2, 3, 4, 5, 6, 7. Now, which of those numbers can be divided evenly by 2?

PUPIL: All of them.

TEACHER: Try again. And this time, *think*.

PUPIL (after a pause): All of them.

TEACHER: All right, how do you divide 5 evenly by 2?

PUPIL: Two and a half and two and a half.

TEACHER: If you're going to be smart-alecky, you can leave the room.

The story is, I am sorry to say, a true one. So is the story of the high school student who was asked on an examination to describe a method for finding the height of a building by using a barometer. The student, bright enough to be bored by the obvious answer, decided to describe not one but two alternate methods. Take the barometer, he wrote, and drop it from the top of the building, timing the interval until you see it smash on the ground. Then, using the standard formula for acceleration of a falling object, calculate the height of the building. Or, he went on, find the owner of the building and say to him, "If you'll tell me how tall your building is I'll give you a good barometer." At last report the student was in deep trouble with his school's administrative hierarchy.

Intelligence is, of course, not a problem just to the young. A study at the University of Michigan revealed that executives with high I.Q.s are as likely to create problems as to solve them—to stumble over their own brains, as one report expressed it. Businessmen with only average I.Q.s, on the other hand, being less apt to confuse themselves with a multiplicity of factors, are often much better problem solvers.

Similarly, psychologist Max L. Fogel, a specialist

14

in intelligence, reports that his studies of Mensa members reveal that being unusually bright can be a distinct problem. "As a group," he writes, "they tend to change jobs more often and encounter more difficulties and dissatisfactions than the general population. This is partly a function of their own personality problems, but it frequently also derives from the belligerence and hostility of employers, peers, and subordinates. Another factor is boredom with established routine and insufficiently creative demands required by vocational responsibilities. . . . Many Mensa members learned to adapt by repressing or disguising their intellectual interests."

Intelligence can cause trouble, too, by teasing the mind into supposing it can solve problems that in fact may defy solution. One bright man, a person who on occasion enjoys a drink or two, addressed himself to the problem of losing weight while continuing to drink, with, in his own words, the following results:

"Losing weight, of course, is a matter of burning up more calories than you take in. A calorie, as everyone knows, is defined as 'the amount of heat required to raise the temperature of one gram of water one degree centigrade.'

"Let us take a good glass of Scotch and soda. Since a gram of water is pretty close to 1 cc (to make it simple), put in plenty of ice and fill it up to about six or seven ounces, making it, say, 200 cc. Since it contains melting ice, its temperature must be 0° centigrade (neglecting the temperature-lowering effect of the alcohol, Scotch, and gas).

"Sooner or later the body must furnish 7400 calories

GAMES FOR THE SUPERINTELLIGENT

(200 cc × 37° C.) to bring it up to body temperature. Since the calorie-counter books show Scotch as 100 calories per shot, and club soda as 0 calories, we should be able to sit around all day, drinking Scotch and soda, and losing weight like mad.

"P.S.: I tried this and it didn't work." So much for the power of pure reason.

On the other hand, being bright does have some undeniable pleasures, and it is one especially beguiling subspecies of those pleasures that this book is all about.

But how can you tell whether these mental pushups and deep knee bends are for you? And how serious a symptom is it if they aren't?

It's a good idea, first of all, to remember that intelligence isn't any single, readily definable quality. On the contrary, it is a complicated assortment of qualities. Some of us possess some of them, some of us others. Columnist Sidney J. Harris has long campaigned against intelligence tests on precisely those grounds—that too many of them treat intelligence as if it were a single identifiable thing, like red hair or double-jointed thumbs. He writes: "We have categorized and stereotyped people for too long by conventional I.Q. tests, which are misleading and inaccurate. Even Binet, the inventor of the first such test, when asked point-blank what intelligence was, replied with cynical candor, 'It is what my test measures.' Of course, as he knew, this is a circular and meaningless definition." Harris, pointing out that a newly devised British test measures six separate abilities (reasoning, verbal ability, spatial perception, number ability, memory, and something called ideational fluency, goes

16

on to say: "I should not be complaining about I.Q. tests because my kind of intelligence does best at them —the highly verbal intelligence. But, knowing how dumb I am in some other important areas of life, it seems to me that the single-score test is profoundly unfair to other equally useful kinds of intelligence. Its abolition can go a long way toward releasing children from the tyranny of a senseless number."

As Harris indicates, a person may possess one mental ability in sharply heightened form but nevertheless be perfectly average in other respects. (Or even, for that matter, considerably below average. Consider the curious case of so-called idiots savants—the hospital patient with the 60 I.Q. who can beat doctors, psychologists, and technicians at checkers, the man with the 29 I.Q. who can instantly calculate the day of the week for any date from 1959 to 1979, or the man with the 30 I.Q. who, having heard any song once, can play it flawlessly on his guitar.) So if you don't particularly enjoy the kind of puzzles and problems we're talking about here, that fact alone says nothing about your intelligence in general. It merely means that you don't have the proper sort of mind for them and that, bright though you may be, you will be happier sticking to bridge, Monopoly, or whatever your special intellectual addiction is. No hard feelings.

But what, exactly, *is* the proper sort of mind? And how do you know if yours is one of them?

Let's start by taking a look at a few of the minds that unquestionably are the sort we are talking about.

Bostock Hackett III, one of the people who contributed to this book, certainly has such a mind. In a letter, he writes of the "thrill" of mental exercise. "In the same manner that an athlete enjoys his conditioning and the feeling of satisfaction that comes from being in shape," he observes, "I have seen [bright people] deliberately create a faster game of Ping Pong in their conversations. The difference between their conversations and those of so-called average people is in the speed, quickness, and agility of the replies." (For some time Hackett has been trying to drum up interest in some sort of "Mental Olympics"—he doesn't specify exactly how it might work—but so far has found no takers.)

Easy Sloman qualifies, too. Here's the kind of thing he enjoys puzzling over:

What is the next letter in the following sequence:

O T T F F S S? (Chapter I, Question 1*)

"That," Sloman says, "is the kind of question I like best. The most fun is not in simple cerebration but in exercising the kind of sideways approach to logic that is not reducible to formula."

An illuminating description of the same phenomenon—the sideways approach—occurs in Arthur Koestler's book *The Act of Creation*. Discussing what happens when no apparent solution to a problem exists, when there is, as he calls it, a "blocked situation," he writes: "When all hopeful attempts at solving the problem by traditional methods have been exhausted, thought runs around in circles . . . like rats in a cage. Next, the matrix of organized, purposeful behavior itself seems to go to pieces, and random trials make their appearance, accompanied by tantrums and attacks of

---

* Answers to puzzles begin on page 105.

despair—or by the distracted absentmindedness of the creative obsession. That absentmindedness is, of course, in fact singlemindedness; for at this stage—the 'period of incubation'—the whole personality, down to the unverbalized and unconscious layers, has become saturated with the problem. . . . This condition remains until either chance or intuition provides a link to a quite different matrix." It is then, and only then, that the problem can be solved.

Some people seem to have a greater talent than others for exercising this sort of sideways logic—for thinking in quite unexpected and essentially unchartable ways. Colin Carmichael, writing in the magazine *Design*, tells the story—it recalls, in a way, our earlier barometer story—of a class of engineering students who were given the following question on an exam: How long should a three-pound beef roast stay in a 325-degree oven for the center to reach a temperature of 150 degrees? One student, described as a "Big Project man," didn't come up with an answer but did offer a plan for a series of precise experiments that would yield an accurate answer in six to nine months. Another student, an advocate of the practical approach, went out and bought a roast, an oven thermometer, and a watch. He wrote his report while munching medium-rare roast beef sandwiches. A third student used logic. Reasoning that animal tissue is mostly water and therefore should have about the same specific heat and conductivity, he applied heat transfer theory to produce his answer (it proved, incidentally, to be quite close to that of the second student). The quickest answer, however, came from a student who called up his mother on the phone and got the answer from her. "Which of these men," asks Mr. Carmichael, "promises to be the most effective engineer?"

What we are talking about is aptly expressed in William P. Hull's description of the thinker: "His delight is in ideas." Many people, for example, find delight in curious logical relationships—such as the oddly useless sign bearing these words:

KEEP OFF THIS SIGN

Or by the card with the intriguing words on both sides. On one side is written:

THE STATEMENT ON THE OTHER SIDE OF THIS CARD IS FALSE.

And on the other side:

THE STATEMENT ON THE OTHER SIDE OF THIS CARD IS TRUE.

(In somewhat the same vein, when Leo Tolstoy and his brother were children they used to pretend that any wish they made would come true if they could stand in a corner and not think of a white bear.)

A student named Norris F. Krueger, Jr., delights in ideas, too—with a sly and cunning difference. "I have a little game I play," he writes. "It's called 'Beat the Establishment.' It goes like this: Someone poses a situation utterly impossible to solve—then we solve it. Sometimes it's a physical problem, like how to retrieve a pencil from some difficult place (such as my principal's office). Sometimes it's purely mental (along the lines of the old argument about how many angels could stand on the head of a pin). This game combines brain-storming, group therapy, and high adventure. (Note: One ground rule is that we proceed through 100 per cent legal methods—no crime, just sneakiness.)"

Or consider the kind of game represented by the apparently simple question:

How many times does the digit 9 appear from 1 to 100? (Puzzle 2)

Think carefully. No, the answer isn't 10. It isn't even 11. If that one has a certain charm for you—and if you stick with it long enough to discover the "hidden" 9's—you're one of us.

Finally, consider the following diagram:

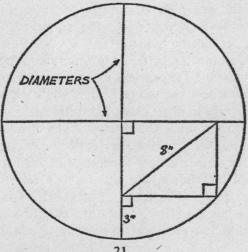

The problem: To find the radius of the circle. (Puzzle 3)

"This problem intrigues me," writes E. C. Hanford, "because the elementary answer is so often reduced to its most complicated form."

This phenomenon—making inherently simple things complicated—is one that has frequently been observed where the minds of very bright people are concerned. Many problems are in fact quite simple but are made difficult because they look, somehow, as if they just *ought* to be difficult, or because the mind is lured into concentrating on an irrelevant aspect of the problem. (I remember, as a child, my wonderment upon first encountering the bus trick: You are told that a bus starts out in the morning with no passengers. At the first stop, three passengers get on. At the next stop, one gets off and two get on. At the next, two get off and one gets on. And so on through several more stops—at which point you are asked: "How many times did the bus stop?")

Jim Cochrane, a particularly inventive puzzle specialist, writes: "There seems to be an interesting class of problematical recreations which, while mathematical in nature, tend to elude the mathematician more often than the non-mathematician. The characteristic of such problems is that they are amenable to solution through methodical application of mathematical tools and techniques, but also may be solved via a short-cut route. The trained mathematician is likely to attack the problem as a specific case of a general problem he has been trained to solve. A child, lacking powerful mathematical tools, is more apt to find the short-cut solution if there is one, since he is forced to take a fresh and creative view. The ability to find the quick solution is probably related to creativity."

A person's feelings about puzzles and games like these are, I think, a fairly reliable touchstone to the presence or absence of certain qualities of mind. If you find that you like them, if they give you an indefinable but quite wonderful sense of pleasure, then you're no doubt right for this book. And it, with luck, will be right for you.

II.

Puzzles and games to start
going quietly crazy by

The typical puzzle, especially the kind most admired by the superintelligent, has its roots in mathematics, in one or another variety of logic, or in words, or it may be based on a combination of these. The puzzles in this chapter, intended as an introduction to the fine art of puzzlemanship, offer a pleasantly maddening *mélange* of those three elements. Practically all of them, incidentally, are from the personal collections of people who are brighter than 98 per cent of the population. So be forewarned: Few of them are easy. But they do constitute a useful Baedeker to the landscape of puzzling.

Let's begin with a couple of quick ones (but not necessarily easy ones):

1. Match Tricks

(a) Make the following equation correct by moving only one match:

(b) And the following:

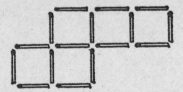

2. Squares and Triangles

Make two squares and four triangles from eight matches, without breaking or bending them.

3. Your Move

Move two matches and make four squares, one of them larger than the other three.

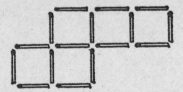

4. Double Cross

The Equality Steamship Company is famous for the unfailing punctuality of its sailings. Every day at noon, Greenwich time, one of its liners leaves Southampton for New York and exactly at the same hour, also

Greenwich time, another boat sails from New York to Southampton. The crossing, in either direction, takes seven days. Thus, whenever an Equality ship departs either from New York or from Southampton, another ship of the same line is just docking there, having arrived from the opposite direction. The eastbound and westbound liners ply the same course. If we board such a vessel at Southampton, how many Equality ships do we meet during our voyage to New York?

5. Shifting the Square

Starting with the position of the pieces at left, move them in such a way as to place the large square A in the position at right. It must, of course, be done without removing any of the pieces. (*Note:* This one, because of the many moves involved, cannot be done as a purely mental problem but should be constructed of cardboard or plywood, with a rectangular frame to insure that the player stays within bounds.)

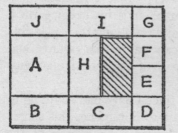 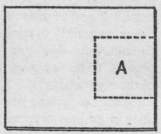

6. Secret Code

Leo Michael Linehan, a onetime cryptographer, describes a game that grows out of his interest in codes:

29

"One game that I often enjoy comes from recasting paragraphs in numerals according to the phone dial. Most people are already familiar with the layout:

2	3	4	5	6	7	8	9
A	D	G	J	M	P	T	W
B	E	H	K	N	R	U	X
C	F	I	L	O	S	V	Y

For Q and Z, I use 1, and 0 will serve for the spaces between words if you want to give yourself that advantage.

"I write my numerals down on a little pad and put it in my pocket. Then, in idle minutes, when I have safely forgotten the clear texts, I fish it out and try to reconstruct the words.

"This, of course, is not unlike deciphering a simple substitution cryptogram, except that a numeral may stand for any of three letters. It is by keeping these letters constantly in mind and revolving their plausible combinations that you can catch the words and phrases. (This is a great part of the intuitive activity of the cryptanalyst.)

"It has been a long time since I have had anything to do with serious cryptography. Sometimes this simple and sedate little exercise brings back a little of the absorption and *joie de faire* that I remember. But of course it is important to use texts that are trifling and uninteresting, the sort of thing you never notice and are unlikely to recall inadvertently in the middle of your game."

Try this one:
71827464084302472530470776252463304676774253028809428036370467677425306326046062843628427084303477807832608377350860276770843028526842022774330270727806304870227460202665084280776833048092704676774253036702078326083773508602767702698446406824053770843028526842

7. In Your Cups

Take a long piece of string and thread it through the handle of a teacup, exactly as shown, and tie the free ends to something. Can the cup be removed from the string without cutting it or undoing the knot?

8. The "Impossible" Problem

Just a glance at this problem is enough to reveal that it is impossible to move the block from the left-hand loop to the right-hand loop (without, of course, untying the rope), for the block is too big to fit through the hole in the bar. But *is* it really impossible?

9. Chess Variations

Chess, absorbing as that game can be, can also be dull unless both players are fairly equally matched. Since it isn't always possible to find an opponent who is your equal, F. C. MacKnight has collected a number of chess variations that render normal knowledge of the game unnecessary or invalid. His descriptions follow:

a. *Replacement chess.* Men are not removed from the board. When captures are made the pieces are replaced on the board at a position chosen by the player who makes the capture. One must win by effectively cutting off the enemy king from his own forces.

b. *Progression chess.* Pawns do not "queen" but instead increase in power as they advance. The pawn on the fifth rank has the movement of the knight, on the sixth of a bishop, on the seventh of a rook, on the eighth of a queen. Moving backward, it loses its power the same way. Otherwise the game is played the same as standard chess.

c. *Check*. The winner is the first to give a simple check; mate is not necessary. The games are usually quite short.

d. *Addition chess*. Another variety of progressive chess where the progression is in the number of moves. White opens with one move, Black takes two moves. White makes three, Black four, and so forth.

e. *Cylindrical chess*. The board is imagined to be a cylinder with the edges adjoining, pieces slipping freely from one side of the board to the other. There are, in other words, no side edges.

f. *Secret arrangement of pieces*. A screen is placed at the midpoint of the board and each player arranges his men as he chooses.

10. Lineup
Draw four connected lines, without retracing your path, that pass through all the points:

11. Super-Categories

The game of Categories is fairly well known, observes the same F. C. MacKnight, but not everyone knows that there are more intricate ways to play it:

"In the commonest form of Categories, one player chooses something and the rest try to find out what it is by asking questions which can be answered by yes or no. Sometimes it is called Animal-Vegetable-Mineral or Twenty Questions, but this is only an elementary variety played by those who cannot think of anything but objects easily placeable in space, and it isn't very good since immaterial things or abstractions cannot be rightly placed in any of these three categories. If you're working on something like the 'reflection of the full moon in the eye of the werewolf on a mountaintop of the Carpathians on Walpurgisnacht' (one I remember pleasurably solving), you don't get it in twenty questions. Or the 'concept of justice in the mind of Felix Frankfurter when he wrote his analysis of the Sacco-Vanzetti case.' Thus there should be no limit on the number of questions, or on the type of category. Variations of these games, which are numerous, usually involve some restriction, such as confining the play to places, people, cartoon characters, actors, etc."

12. Rugged Challenge

You have a 9 × 12-foot rug with an 8 × 1-foot hole in the middle. Cut the rug into two pieces (no more and no less) so that the two pieces can be sewn together to make a solid 10 × 10-foot rug.

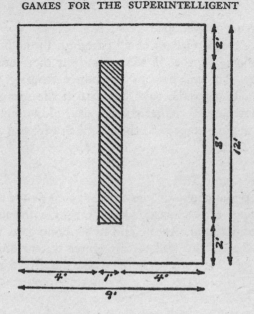

13. The Spider and the Fly

A 12 × 30-foot room has a 12-foot ceiling. In the middle of the end wall, a foot above the floor, is a spider. The spider wants to capture a fly in the middle of the opposite wall, one foot below the ceiling. What is the shortest path the spider can take?

14. Ups and Downs

A snail is at the bottom of a well 30 feet deep. It can crawl upward 3 feet in one day, but at night it slips back 2 feet. How long does it take the snail to crawl out of the well?

15. Jarring Experience

There are two jars of equal capacity. In the first jar there is one amoeba. In the second jar there are two amoebas. An amoeba can reproduce itself in three minutes. It takes the two amoebas in the second jar three hours to fill the jar to capacity. How long does it take the one amoeba in the first jar to fill that jar to capacity?

16. Time and Tide

A ship is at anchor. Over its side hangs a rope ladder with rungs a foot apart. The tide rises at the rate of 8 inches per hour. At the end of six hours how much of the rope ladder will remain above water, assuming that 8 feet were above water when the tide began to rise?

17. Case of the Clever Cook

A camp cook wants to measure four ounces of vinegar out of a jug, but he has only a five-ounce and a three-ounce container. How can he do it?

18. The Splintered Circle

What is the maximum number of parts into which a circle may be divided by drawing four straight lines?

19. Fast

A race driver drove around a 6-mile track at 140 mph for three miles, 168 mph for 1½ miles, and 210 mph for 1½ miles. What was his average speed for the entire 6 miles?

20. Catching Up

A truck travels 15 mph for the first half of the distance of a trip. How fast must it travel in the second half of the distance in order to average 30 mph for the total trip?

21. Sprouts

This game, played by two or more people, begins with a number of dots, preferably from three to ten. Taking turns, the players draw curves from dot to dot, each time putting a dot on the new line. The maximum permissible number of rays from each dot is three. The last one to draw a curve and dot wins. Here is how a game between two players, starting with five dots, might look:

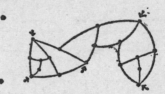

22. Cubes

Start off by drawing a cube (or, if you have them, use children's blocks). There is obviously only one way a single cube can be arranged—

so this is the end of the first series.

Next, do the same thing with two cubes. The results

are identical—there is only one way to put them together:

With three cubes, there are two possible ways they may be arranged:

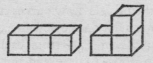

With four cubes there are seven ways:

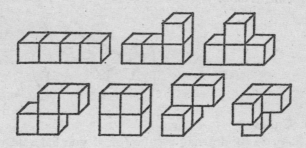

As for the rules, the only one is that cubes must abut face to face. The real puzzle is to find a formula for calculating the number of possible combinations for a given number of cubes. "Unfortunately," writes Alan E. Thompson, who invented the game, "I am not sure that there is such a rule. I think it probable that a computer would be needed once you got above the next two series." Anyone care to try?

23. Psychological Jujitsu

In this game all you need are unflinching nerves and an ability to think one jump ahead of your opponent when he's trying to do exactly the same thing to you. Required are the spade, club, and heart suits of a deck of cards. King counts 13, Queen 12, Jack 11, Ace 1, and all number cards count their number. Suits are of no consequence.

The object of the game is to win the greatest number of hearts. Player A takes the spade suit, player B the club suit. The hearts are shuffled, cut, and placed in a stack, face down, between the players.

Play begins with a heart being turned up from the top of the stack. Player A and player B each select one of their cards, placing it face down on the table. They then turn their cards over, and the player with the higher card wins the heart. This sequence is repeated for each of the thirteen tricks.

Each spade or club may be played only once, after which the cards are left face up, to remove all advantage of memory. If there is a tie on a play, the value of that card is split; the easiest way to accomplish that is to take the card out of the count. Forty-six heart points win.

As to possible strategies, there are three: Play to each heart at random; play a predetermined value for each heart; or determine your play as each heart turns up. Since both players start even, the winner wins by virtue of his ability to outthink his opponent. He wins, that is, by guessing what his opponent will, in effect, bid for a heart and then either trying to beat him by only one point or to lose by a lot.

Note: This is a superb game for children. Aside from being fun, it teaches them very quickly that life is complicated, unpredictable, and, all too often, terribly unfair.

24. Perspective

Kurt Nassau supplies a puzzle involving engineering drawings. In such drawings, the use of solid and dotted lines is most easily explained by an illustration—three views and a perspective drawing of the same object:

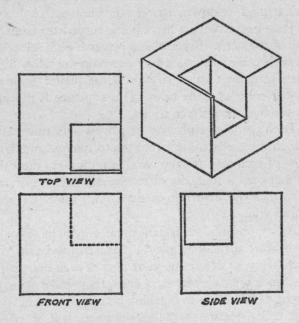

TOP VIEW

FRONT VIEW

SIDE VIEW

Now look at these two views of a different object:

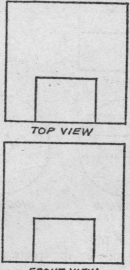

TOP VIEW

FRONT VIEW

What is the side view like? A perspective view?

25. Circles and a Square

Also from an engineer's drawing board, here's one I might never have figured out had not a kindly engineer friend taken pity on me and made me a small model of it. (It goes well on a key chain.) What is the shape depicted?

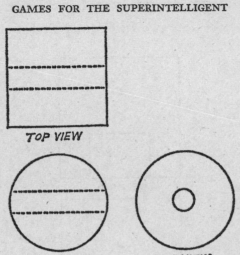

TOP VIEW

FRONT VIEW   SIDE VIEW

26. Matches in Rows

This one, to judge by the frequency with which it turns up in the archives of the superintelligent, is a special favorite. It appears to be simple, but the underlying principle eludes most people who try to analyze it.

The game is played with matches, which are placed in three rows. The top row has three matches, the second five matches, and the third seven matches. The object of the game is to make your opponent remove the last match.

The rules are as follows:

1. Players alternate moves.

2. Matches may be removed from only one row at a time.

3. Any number of matches may be removed by either player on his move, provided he takes from only one row at a time.

The game is played on the basis of "losing combinations." Each player tries to leave his opponent with such a combination. Once any of the losing combinations is given to your opponent he cannot win; losing combinations with the larger numbers of matches can simply be reduced to those made up of smaller numbers.

The game, as mentioned, starts with the combination 3-5-7. The losing combinations are:

2-5-7
3-4-7
3-5-6
1-4-5
1-2-3
1-1-1

An even number in any two rows

If he knows these combinations, the person to move first can assure his victory simply by removing one match from any of the three rows. His opponent has lost before he has even begun.

III.

Words to the wise
(and from them, too)

For many of the superintelligent, word games are to be preferred above all other types of puzzles. One reason is that extremely bright people are, by definition, verbally adept people. Typically they have a way of noticing, delighting in, and remembering words that other people are likely to ignore or forget, and they are ordinarily very good at any challenge involving words. Though a very bright person may have seen words like *eyot* and *orrery* only once in his lifetime, he remembers what they mean when he encounters them again.* He knows, too, what six-letter word contains three y's** and what common English word has no rhyme.*** Beyond all that, he has a general verbal facility that makes playing word games and solving word puzzles as natural for him and as much fun as it is for Vida Blue to throw a baseball.

The fun comes in four main forms:

1. Tests and questions (like those above).

* Eyot: an islet or small island. Orrery: a device for illustrating the motions of the planets.
** Syzygy.
*** Orange.

47

2. Standard games, such as Scrabble, Perquackey, crossword puzzles, and double-crostics.

3. Made-up games, like Definitions (see below).

4. Just-messing-around games (also discussed below).

Let's look at some examples of each—and, in some cases, some inventive variations.

TESTS AND QUESTIONS

I have been collecting these, on odd scraps of paper, for years and have a good-sized collection ranging from the very simple to the quite difficult. Judge for yourself which of the following is which:

1. What eight-letter word contains only one vowel?

2. What word contains all five vowels in alphabetical order?

3. What word contains three sets of double letters in a row?

4. Punctuate the following so it makes sense: *John while James had had had had had had had had had had had a better effect on the teacher*.

What do the following words have in common: *deft, first, calmness, canopy, laughing, stupid, crabcake, hijack* (Puzzle 5). Jim Cochrane, commenting on first encountering this question, writes, "This one was bad for my ego. After I stared at it for five minutes or so, my wife, Carolyn, walked over, laughed, and informed me that it was obvious. I saw it several minutes later."

Finally, here is, in my opinion the world's most deceptively difficult spelling test—five perfectly ordinary English words that even many professional editors and writers fail to score a passing 60 per cent on. (*Stop!* Don't spoil it by looking; have someone read them to you.)

Inoculate
Iridescent
Rarefy
Kimono
Naphtha

STANDARD GAMES

As mentioned, these include such games as Scrabble, Perquackey, crossword puzzles, and double-crostics, all of them games with great appeal for many of the superintelligent. Characteristically, however, the superintelligent add special wrinkles of their own to increase the challenge. For example, in college I knew a kindly old government professor and Scrabble aficionado whose secret goal was to use words that were ever so slightly risqué. The high point of our series of matches, which went on over a number of years, was his triumphant spelling of *brassiere*, an accomplishment that not only earned him fifty extra points for using all seven of his tiles ("re" was already on the board) but also abundantly satisfied his special verbal idiosyncrasy.

Similarly, Perquackey, a game wonderfully suited to people of all ages from seven or eight upward, can be made into an equal contest for opponents of quite different abilities if the better player is simply required to use fewer of the lettered dice. When my ten-year-old son, John, and I play each other, he gains a slight advantage by using the three red dice, in addition to the seven black ones, while I must spell only with the black ones. Played that way, our games usually turn out to be remarkably close.

When it comes to crossword puzzles and double-crostics, I confess to an unaccountable blind spot. I am absolutely no good at either. In fact, I stand awed and humbled in the presence of a man like Henry Bate of Riverside, Connecticut, who on the morning commuter train likes to postpone doing the New York *Times* crossword puzzle until he has reached the 125th Street station. Then he races, usually without a flaw, through the whole puzzle in the nine or ten minutes between there and Grand Central. (During that time, of course, one attempts to engage Mr. Bate in conversation only at one's own peril.)

Still, I am open-minded enough to see that crosswords and double-crostics have proved pleasantly addictive to many, so I include here one of the more difficult of the former (Puzzle 6). It was composed by a fiendishly intelligent gentleman named N. A. S. Vincent, who is head of the Mathematics Department at Greenhill County Secondary School in Tenby, England. In offering it to me for use in this book, Mr. Vincent made the following confessional comment: "I used this crossword to round off a lesson on 'shape' with a General Studies sixth form. None of the class completed it, so I have provided some hints and answers. Some of the clues, I will agree, are contrived, but it gave an immense amount of pleasure and stimulated interest."

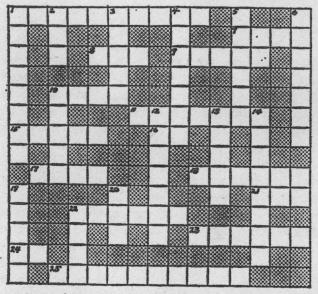

ACROSS

1. II
7. C
8. ✝
9. △
10. EEEE
11. ꓕꓒ
15. /A
16. U
17. DR
18. $\overline{G}$
21. UU
22. CC
23. N₂
24. 2
25. Ȯ

DOWN

1. ®
2. π
3. A
4. ℋℰ
5. $\frac{I}{II}$
6. ☼D
10. ↑E
12. MṀ
13. DK
14. R
19. MT
20. ÄO
22. ÄÖ

Well, don't say you weren't warned; I *said* Mr. Vincent was fiendish.

MADE-UP GAMES

Of the making up of games there is no end. On long automobile trips, for example, my wife and children and I play such homemade games as Road Signs (see who can spell the most words with the letters on such signs as MASSACHUSETTS TURNPIKE—¼ MILE AHEAD) and Animals (taking turns, think of animals whose names start with successive letters of the alphabet; *e.g.*, aardvark, bat, cat . . .). Practically everybody has composed games of their own at one time or another, or invented variations of known games, with the result that the precise genealogy of a game is often very difficult, if not downright impossible, to determine.

David Greene Kolodny, for example, describes a game in which the rule of the game is simply to state the rule of the game. The individual may ask questions that can be answered with a yes or a no. The interesting feature of the game is that the literal meaning of the questions is of no significance. The way it goes is this: If the last letter of the last word in the question ends with the letters from A to M, the question is automatically answered with a yes. On the other hand, if the last letter of the last word in the question ends with a letter from N to Z, the question is answered with a no. For example, if the question "Are you lying?" is asked, the answer is yes. If the next question is "Are you telling the truth?" the answer is again yes.

The results can be quite amusing, Mr. Kolodny says. During one game, the questions turned to Dante's *Inferno*. One misguided player, assuming the answer was somehow to be found in that book, read the whole thing twice in an effort to solve the problem.

Another correspondent, Samuel A. Shaffe, confesses himself a partisan of a kind of cryptographic hide-and-seek. Two players each select a word (in this case, they agree to choose five-letter words with no repeated letters). Then, in turn, each player calls out a word and the other player tells how many of the letters in the mystery word are contained in that word. Mr. Shaffe says a sample game—an extremely simple one —might go something like this:

JOHN: My first word is *scene*, s-c-e-n-e. [Repeated letters, like the two *e*'s in *scene*, are not permitted in the secret words but are permitted in the calls.]

MARY: One letter. OK, I'll also say *scene*.

JOHN: You get two. I'll say *stems*.

MARY: You get a big round zero for *stems*. My next word is *steam*.

JOHN: *Steam* gives you four. Are you cheating or something? *Scant* is my word.

MARY: *Scant* gets you one. *Stage* is my next word.

JOHN: *Stage* gets you four again. *Slant*, s-l-a-n-t.

MARY: That's just one. *Least*.

JOHN: *Least* gives you five, but that's not the word. Well, it's hopeless now, but here goes: *tells*.

MARY: *Steal*, s-t-e-a-l. Is that your word?

JOHN: That's it, all right. You've got an LC in yours, but that's no help. What is it?

MARY: *Could*, you dummy. I win again!

Mr. Shaffe points out that the game can be made considerably more complicated by agreeing to choose longer words. Or, if a handicapping system is desired, one player might pick a four-letter word and the other, say, a six-letter word.

Finally, here is another one that has given me particular delight—a variant of the familiar childhood game called Ghost. In Ghost, you will remember, each player adds a letter until someone is forced to end the word. In this game, things are done a bit differently, though the object is still to avoid ending a word. Players alternate in starting with two letters, neither of which can be the first or last letters of the word. Subsequent players add one letter each, either at the beginning or the end. A typical game might go like this:

Player *A:* RD
Player *B:* RDR
Player *A:* ERDR
Player *B:* VERDR
Player *A:* OVERDR
Player *B* (thinking of OVERDRAMATIC): OVERDRA
Player *A* (avoiding the trap): OVERDRAF
Player *B:* OVERDRAFT (loses)

JUST-MESSING-AROUND GAMES

The true wordman can find pleasure practically anywhere anything has been written. He can, for example, have fun speculating on why some of the things in advertisements are written with such inventive ineptitude. I once found myself puzzling, for example, over the wording of an advertisement for sunglasses. The ad showed a boy wearing sunglasses. The headline read: "Look, Ma, I'm glancing at the world through [let's say] Ajax sunglasses." Thinking about the utter wrongness of that word "glancing," which no boy ever uttered in that context and no boy ever will, I thought I saw just what had happened: The copywriter, having written that "Look, Ma," didn't want to use "look" again, so groped for another word. His problem, poor fellow, was that "look" is just about the only right word to use there. What he should have done, of course, is change the first "look." A simple "Hey, Ma" would have done the trick.

Advertising, bless its busily creative heart, is full of such amusements.

Amusements of a different sort may be found in dictionaries, thesauruses, and books of quotations. I remember, for example, reading a magazine article some years ago in which the author, a man fascinated by the oddness of words, described himself as a kind of verbal zookeeper, a collector of strange specimens for no purpose other than to marvel at them. There are, I have since discovered, many such people, people who would rather track down and capture a curious word than the most exotic bird or butterfly.

Rita Schoch Sagers, for example, wonders about such questions as "What is the difference between flammable and inflammable?" And Ethel Wollman (who says "I am especially delighted with the kind of puzzle I can make up myself") offers a collection of definitions that she calls "Malapropossibles." Among them:

Symmetry: an Irish graveyard.

Kitty Hawk: a buzzard that eats cats.

Melancholic: what you get when you eat too much cantaloupe.

Mandate: a rendezvous with a fella.

Infatuate: to put on weight.

Gnu: what you've always known.

Sir Lancelot: a very busy medieval surgeon.

Olfactory: an ancient mill that smells.

Intent: an "at home" when you're on a camping trip.

Inspired by these examples, I came up with one of my own:

Questionable: what the police do when they interrogate a cow's husband.

See? It's easy. (If not always completely painless.) Your turn.

IV.

Those wonderful laws of logic
(and how they can fool
you every time)

The study of philosophy begins with logic, on the grounds that without clear thought the mind can't do much of anything. At the outset, therefore, students of philosophy learn such useful principles as the fact that a thing cannot simultaneously be A and not A, that syllogisms must follow a certain pattern in order to be valid, and that to find fault with a person is not the same as finding fault with his argument. After a brief immersion in this sort of thing, the student may be forgiven if he begins to think he has acquired some quite potent instruments for validating truth and sniffing out error. And of course he has—provided other people play the game by the rules and agree not to use *ad hominem* arguments, not to be deliberately misleading (40 per cent more effective than *what?*), not to sulk, not to pound fists and shoes on the table, and not to bully each other with patriotic slogans and full-page ads in *Life*. The trouble, as we all know, is that such agreements never stay in effect for long. No, the fact is that we often set out *deliberately* to mislead each other, with results familiar to us all.

This chapter consists of some of the pleasanter, more harmless examples of such attempts to mislead, or at least to force the victim to use something beyond mere plodding, dogged logic. For it will be seen at once that these puzzles have one thing in common: Not a single one of them will yield up its secret to mere diligence or persistence; at least a pinch of brilliance must be thrown in. Every one of them, in other words, requires some leap of logic that must sometimes be merely clever and sometimes dazzlingly brilliant. But it must always be considerably more than all but the superintelligent (and perhaps a few of their closest intellectual kin) can muster.

1. Warmup

This is an old one but still a good one. (Max Batchelder, a member of Mensa and a puzzle enthusiast, calls it "my all-time favorite.") It takes many different forms, as virtually all the old favorites among puzzles do; here it is as Mr. Batchelder gives it:

"A hunter arose early, ate breakfast, and headed south. Half a mile from camp he tripped and skinned his nose. He picked himself up, cursing, and continued south. Half a mile farther along, he spotted a bear. Drawing a bead, he pulled the trigger, but the safety was on. The bear saw him and headed east at top speed. Half a mile later the hunter caught up, fired, but only wounded the beast, which limped on toward the east. The hunter followed and half a mile later caught and killed the bear. Pleased, the hunter walked the mile north back to his camp to find it had been ransacked by a second bear.

"What color was the bear that tore up his camp?"

The clues are all there.

2. Cutting Up

A carpenter wants to cut a cube of wood into 27 equal cubes. It is obvious that he can accomplish this with six cuts:

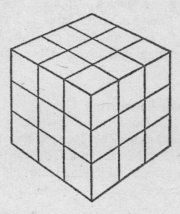

Is there any procedure that would require fewer than six cuts? If there is, describe it. If there isn't, explain why not.

3. Taking Sides

Given: Four pieces of cardboard. You are told that each one is either red or green on one side, and that each one has either a circle or a square on the other side. They appear on the table as follows:

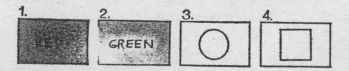

Which ones must you pick up and turn over in order

to have sufficient information to answer the question: Does every red one have a square on its other side?

4. No Peeking

Three boxes are labeled "Apples," "Oranges," and "Apples and Oranges." Each label is incorrect. You may select only one fruit from one box. (No feeling around or peeking permitted.) How can you label each box correctly?

5. Case of the Counterfeit Coin

You have twelve identical-looking coins, one of which is counterfeit. The counterfeit coin is either heavier or lighter than the rest. The only scale available is a simple balance. Using the scale only three times, find the counterfeit coin.

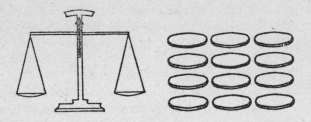

6. True or False?

A missionary visits an island where two tribes live. One tribe always tells the truth. The other always lies. The truth tellers live on the western side of the island and the liars live on the eastern side of the island. The missionary's problem is to determine who tells the truth by asking one native only one question.

The missionary, seeing a native walking in the distance, asks a nearby native: "Go ask that native in the distance which side of the island he lives on." When the messenger returns he answers: "He says he lives on the western side of the island." Is the messenger a truth teller or a liar? How can you be sure?

7. More Natives

In the South Pacific, so the story goes, white people get sunburned to a brown color that is identical to the native islanders' color. There is only one way to tell them apart: by what they say. Islanders always lie. Non-islanders always tell the truth.

A visitor is paddling a canoe up to the beach of an island when he sees three people, all the same brown color. He asks, "Are you white people burned brown or are you islanders?" The first one calls out something that is lost in the sound of the surf, so the man in the canoe again shouts, "Are you islanders or sunburned white people?"

This time the second man on the beach calls back, saying, "The first person who answered said he is a white man, and he *is* a white man, and so am I." The third person on the beach called out, "The first two people here on the beach are islanders and I am a white man burned brown."

From what they have said, tell what each man really is.

8. Dog Days

This one is tough but can be solved by a strict application of logic (provided you've got a goodly amount of serendipity to go along with it). It comes from Irving Hale, who describes it this way:

"This 'cross-number puzzle' was given to me by a secretary at the bank where I formerly was employed. I don't know where she got it but it is obviously English and around thirty years old. It is a marvelous problem. Solving it requires a well-balanced combination of logic, calculation, and trial-and-error. The numbers are so interlocked that practically every one of them must be employed in reaching the final entry (2 down.)

"The puzzle concerns a farm that has been in the Dunk family for some years. A part of the farm is a rectangular piece of ground known as Dog's Mead. Additional background information: The year is 1939; 4840 square yards = one acre; 4 roods = one acre."

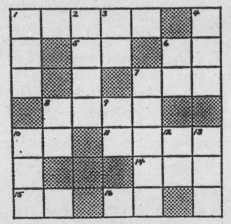

Across

1. Area in square yards of Dog's Mead
5. Age of Martha, Father Dunk's aunt
6. Difference in yards between length and breadth of Dog's Mead
7. Number of roods in Dog's Mead times 8 down
8. The year the Dunks acquired Dog's Mead
10. Father Dunk's age
11. Year of Mary's birth
14. Perimeter in yards of Dog's Mead
15. Cube of Father Dunk's walking speed in mph
16. 15 across minus 9 down

Down

1. Value in shillings per rood of Dog's Mead
2. Square of the age of Father Dunk's mother-in-law
3. Age of Mary, Father Dunk's other daughter
4. Value in pounds of Dog's Mead
6. Age of Ted, Father Dunk's son, who is twice the age of his sister Mary in 1945
7. Square of the breadth of Dog's Mead
8. Time in minutes it takes Father Dunk to walk 1⅓ times around Dog's Mead
9. The number which, multiplied by 10 across, gives 10 down
10. See 9 down
12. Addition of the digits of 10 down plus 1
13. Number of years Dog's Mead has been in the Dunk family

9. Theirs to Reason Why

The same Easy Sloman mentioned in Chapter 1 has sent me his version of one of the most popular of all logic puzzles. It is, in fact, so popular and—to true aficionados—so common that at least one friend has urged me not to mention it again for fear of driving readers away. I think it's a wonderful puzzle, though, no matter how familiar, so here it is:

Three intelligent men, applying for a job, seem equal in all pertinent attributes, so the prospective employer, also an intelligent man, sets a simple problem for them. The job, he says, will go to the first applicant to solve it. A mark is placed on each man's forehead. The three are told that each has either a black mark or a white mark, and each is to raise his hand if he sees a black mark on the forehead of either of the other two. The first one to tell what color he has and how he arrived at his answer will get the job. Each man raised his hand, and after a few seconds one man comes up with the answer. What color was his mark, and how did he figure it out?

10. Variation

If you think *that* one is hard, consider the same problem with not just three but *four* job applicants. All four are told that they are exceptionally intelligent. They are, in fact, all familiar with the three-person puzzle (above), and each knows that the other three are familiar with it, too. They are asked two questions: Anyone who can see two black marks is to stand up; and anyone who knows the color of the mark on his own forehead is to raise his hand. All four men stand up. Then, after a few minutes, one of them raises his hand and correctly announces the color of his mark. What was it and how did he know?

11. Love Story

Four men and four women are shipwrecked on a desert island. Eventually each one falls in love with one other, and is himself loved by one person. John falls in love with a girl who is, unfortunately, in love with Jim. Arthur loves a girl who loves the man who loves Ellen. Mary is loved by the man who is loved by the girl who is loved by Bruce. Gloria hates Bruce and is hated by the man whom Hazel loves. Who loves Arthur?

12. Zoo Story

MAN: How many birds and how many beasts do you have in your zoo?
ZOOKEEPER: There are 30 heads and 100 feet.
MAN: I can't tell from *that*.
ZOOKEEPER: Oh, yes you can!
Can *you?*

13. Batter Up!

Andy dislikes the catcher. Ed's sister is engaged to the second baseman. The center fielder is taller than the right fielder. Harry and the third baseman live in the same building. Paul and Allen each won $20 from the pitcher at pinochle. Ed and the outfielders play poker during their free time. The pitcher's wife is the third baseman's sister. The pitcher, catcher, and infielders except Allen, Harry, and Andy, are shorter than Sam. Paul, Andy and the shortstop lost $50 each at the racetrack. Paul, Harry, Bill, and the catcher took a trouncing from the second baseman at pool. Sam is involved in a divorce suit. The catcher and the third baseman each have two children. Ed, Paul, Jerry, the right fielder, and the center fielder are bachelors. The others are married. The shortstop, the third baseman, and Bill each cleaned up $100 betting on the fight. One of the outfielders is either Mike or Andy. Jerry is taller than Bill. Mike is shorter than Bill. Each of them is heavier than the third baseman.

Using these facts, determine the names of the men playing the various positions on the baseball team.

14. Bang

Two automobiles are approaching each other at a constant velocity of 60 mph. When the autos are two miles apart, a very fast fly leaves the front bumper of one of the autos and travels toward the other at a speed of 120 mph. Upon reaching that auto, the fly immediately reverses direction. This continues until the autos collide (or, to make it less gory, let's say narrowly *miss* colliding). How far did the fly travel?

15. Checkmate

A standard chessboard is truncated by removing two corner squares diagonally opposite each other. Can thirty-one dominoes, each able to cover two adjacent squares, be used to cover all sixty-two squares of the truncated chessboard? If so, how? If not, why not?

16. Question

A traveler comes to a fork in the road and does not know which way to go to reach his destination. There are two men at the fork, one of whom always lies while the other always tells the truth. The traveler doesn't know which is which. He may ask one of the men only one question to find his way. What is his question and which man does he ask?

17. Probabilities

You have 10 gray socks and 20 blue socks in your bureau drawer. If you reach into it in the dark, how many socks must you take out to be sure of having a pair that matches?

V.

The fine, frustrating art of
numbermanship

If you like puzzles, there is no more pleasant or effective way to while away, say, a long airplane trip than to take along two or three tough, intricate problems and some scratch paper. I did just that not long ago on a flight from New York to Los Angeles and in the process discovered what promptly became my all-time favorite mathematical puzzle. It seems to me to demand just the right combination of logic, intuition, and trial-and-error. Though essentially simple, it is also tricky in its way, each piece of the solution dovetailing with the next like the parts of a Chinese puzzle. There are thousands of mathematical problems—any good library contains a surprising number of books on the subject—but for my money there can never be too many like this one:

1. Multiplying by 4

Supply a digit for each letter so that the equation is correct. There is only one set of digits that will work. A given letter always represents the same digit:

$$
\begin{array}{r}
\text{A B C D E} \\
\times\ 4 \\
\hline
\text{E D C B A}
\end{array}
$$

73

2. Compound Interest
And here's an elegant little addition problem:

$$
\begin{array}{c}
S\ E\ N\ D \\
+\ M\ O\ R\ E \\
\hline
M\ O\ N\ E\ Y
\end{array}
$$

3. Lost and Found
In the rearranged triangle (right), where does the extra square come from?

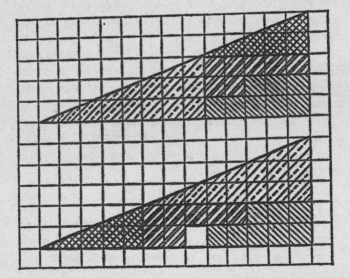

Andrew F. Bender calls this puzzle "the most intriguing I have ever encountered." He says it has "stumped more people than ony other puzzle I know."

4. Missing Number

Supply the missing number in the following sequence:

10
11
12
13
14
15
16
17
20
22
24
31
100
?
10000
1111111111111111

5. Two Buckets

One bucket contains a gallon of water, another a gallon of alcohol. A cup of alcohol from the second bucket is poured into the bucket of water. A cup of the resulting mixture is then poured back into the bucket of alcohol. Is there:

(a) More water in the alcohol than alcohol in the water;

(b) More alcohol in the water than water in the alcohol;

(c) The same amount of water in the alcohol as alcohol in the water?

6. Homeward Bound

Each day a man's wife meets him at the railroad station and drives him home. One day he arrives at the station an hour early and begins to walk home along the road his wife always takes. She meets him en route and takes him the rest of the way home. Had he waited at the station, she would have picked him up exactly on time. As it turned out, he reached his home twenty minutes early. How long did the man walk?

7. Weighty Problem

If you have a balance scale, what is the minimum number of weights that can be used to weigh any number of pounds from one to forty? What are the weights?

8. And now, in ring one . . .

A circus performance is witnessed by 120 people who have paid a total of $120. The men paid $5, the women $2, and the children 10¢ each. How many of each went to the circus?

9. Monkey Business

A rope over the top of a fence has the same length on each side. It weighs one third of a pound per foot. On one end hangs a monkey holding a banana, and on the other end a weight equal to the weight of the monkey. The banana weighs two ounces per inch. The rope is as long (in feet) as the age of the monkey (in years), and the weight of the monkey (in ounces) is the same as the age of the monkey's mother. The combined ages of the monkey and its mother are thirty years. One half the weight of the monkey, plus the weight of the banana, is one fourth as much as the weight of the weight and the weight of the rope. The monkey's mother is half as old as the monkey will be when it is three times as old as its mother was when she was half as old as the monkey will be when it is as old as its mother will be when she is four times as old as the monkey was when it was twice as old as its mother was when she was one third as old as the monkey was when it was as old as its mother was when she was three times as old as the monkey was when it was one fourth as old as it is now. How long is the banana?

10. Bridge into Troubled Waters

A genius came to a narrow railroad bridge and began to run across it. He had crossed three eighths of the distance when a whistle behind him warned of an approaching train. Being a genius, he instantly evaluated his alternatives. If he were to run back to the beginning of the bridge at his speed of 10 mph, he would leave the bridge at precisely the moment the train entered it. If he kept on running to the end of the bridge, the train would reach him just as he left the bridge. At what speed was the train moving?

11. Stringing Along

A man buys a string 25,000 miles long and sets out to stretch it around the circumference of the earth. When he reaches his starting point, he discovers that the string is in fact 25,000 miles and one yard long.

Rather than cut the string, he decides to tie the ends together and distribute the extra 36 inches evenly around the entire circumference. How far does the string stand out from the earth because of the extra yard? (Disregard the length of string used to tie the knot.)

12. Equations That Changed the World

Nicaragua, a country that must be a mathematician's paradise, not long ago issued ten postage stamps bearing LAS 10 FORMULAS MATEMATICAS QUE CAMBIARON LA FAZ DE LA TERRA (The 10 mathematical formulas that changed the face of the world). How many of them can you identify?

(a) $1+1=2$

(b) $f = \dfrac{Gm_1m_2}{r^2}$

(c) $E = mc^2$

(d) $e^{\ln N} = N$

(e) $A^2 + B^2 = C^2$

(f) $S = k \log W$

(g) $V = V_e \ln \dfrac{m_0}{m_1}$

(h) $\lambda = h/mv$

(i) $V^2 E = \dfrac{Ku}{c^2} \dfrac{\delta^2 B}{\delta t^2}$

(j) $F_1 x_1 = F_2 X_2$

13. $3 + 3 = 4$

Here's one that clearly calls for the "sideways approach" that was mentioned earlier, for a moment's reflection will reveal that it cannot be done in any ordinary way. The problem is simply to arrange four pennies so that there are two straight lines with three pennies on each line.

If you can do that one in five minutes or less, then you've thoroughly caught on to the mental phenomena that this book is all about. (Those phenomena are discussed in more specific detail in the following chapter.)

VI.

The superintelligent: how they got
that way and how
they stay that way

In the preceding pages we've been talking a great deal about human intelligence. We've been making some observations about how it works, what it can accomplish and what, if a person doesn't have enough of it, it can't accomplish. This whole book is, in fact, built on the premises that 1) there is indeed something properly identifiable as intelligence and that 2) some people have more of it—in some cases a lot more of it —than others.

But now, in the face of all that, it is also necessary to admit that no one really knows what intelligence is, or even whether there is any objective quality or set of qualities that conforms to our notion of what constitutes intelligence. "How far these 'qualities' represent some objective reality in the personality and how far they are constructs of the human mind in relation to the behavior of the person we are unable to judge," writes Victor Serebriakoff.

In short, no one knows exactly what intelligence is (the only thing we're absolutely certain intelligence tests do is measure what intelligence tests measure), yet we all agree, somehow, that there is such a thing as intelligence. We are all likely to agree, too, that it is parceled out quite unequally among the human species.

Furthermore, it has been shown that I.Q.—which is nothing more than intelligence in relation to an individual's chronological age—has certain typical characteristics. Researchers have discovered, for example, that intelligence normally stops increasing at the beginning of adolescence (except in the case of certain very bright people whose intelligence may continue developing until eighteen or so). This is not to say, however, that the ability to *use* one's intelligence cannot be improved well beyond that time. In fact, if a reader has been diligent enough to work his way this far into this book, he has probably discovered a number of mental techniques that had not previously been in his armamentarium. He is, it is true, fundamentally no more intelligent, but he may be able to *do* more with his intelligence. For that reason his I.Q.—which, remember, is by definition simply what an I.Q. test measures—may actually be slightly higher. And to anyone who watches him unerringly solve an unfamiliar problem he will certainly *look* more intelligent.

There is, therefore, something we can do about improving the *use* of intelligence, though there is considerable room for debate over just how much we can do. (One recent estimate is that 80 per cent of intelligence is nature, only 20 per cent nurture.) One way to improve one's ability to use one's mind is simply to see how very bright people use theirs. Let's look closely at a few of the puzzles that appear in this book with an eye to finding out what the superintelligent do that's different from what ordinary people do.

1. *The OTTFFSS series problem (Chapter I, Question 1).* The solver first tries the most obvious routes —the intervals between the letters, the pattern of single and double letters, and so forth—but finds no clues there. Finally he begins to suspect that he needs to search for an entirely different kind of solution. But what kind? He thinks, perhaps, of such things as the sounds of the letters and their shapes. Nothing there. Finally, still looking for something he now knows must be very different from the more obvious solutions, he asks himself: Do the letters *stand* for something? Persistence alone will now bring its reward, and eventually a thought occurs to him: One, Two, Three . . . !

The key here, I think, is the puzzler's confidence that he has thoroughly examined each possible level of solution before discarding it. As one level proves fruitless, he feels justified in turning his full attention to the next possibility. He does not linger over apparently lost causes.

2. *The four squares problem (II, 3).* Anyone trying to solve this one, whether or not he is extraordinarily bright, will quickly see that it impossible to do what the problem seems at first glance to call for—that is, to make four identical squares out of five by moving just two matches. Trial and error will reveal that much within a minute or two. While the ordinary person is

likely to continue trying to solve it in those terms, the bright person looks for an escape route. What might such a route be? Can the problem be solved by using the third dimension? No, for that would require more than just two matches. Finally it occurs to him that all the squares need not be the same size. With that realization he is suddenly very close to the answer (and to the realization that there is nothing in the problem that says one square can't be inside another). The key question the puzzler needs to ask himself is: "What assumptions about the conditions of the problem am I making that I need not make?" Once he has broken free of two unnecessary assumptions he has the problem solved.

3. *The nine dots problem (II, 10).* Who said the lines had to stay inside the boundaries of the dots? The intelligent person tries, as we saw above, not to impose unnecessary restrictions on his mind.

4. *The apples and oranges puzzle (IV, 4).* Both the ordinary person and the bright person see one thing clearly right away: that if, for example, a fruit is picked from the box marked "Apples," it can be either an apple or an orange and will therefore tell nothing about whether the box should be marked "Oranges" or "Apples and Oranges." Since the same is true if a fruit is picked from the box marked "Oranges," it is tempting to conclude that the same will also be true of the third box, "Apples and Oranges." But the bright person does not take that supposition for granted. In-

stead, he goes ahead and tries it. Suppose, he thinks, I pick a fruit from "Apples and Oranges" and it turns out to be an orange—then what do I know about what's in that box? Well, for one thing, since we have been told that all the boxes are wrongly labeled, we know that it is not "Apples and Oranges." Therefore it must be oranges. Then the remaining boxes contain apples and apples and oranges. But which contains which? Simple. Remember once again that the boxes are all mislabeled. Simply switch the two remaining labels and the problem is solved. The bright person has succeeded because he does not assume the problem cannot be solved simply because it cannot be solved in one way or even two ways he has tried. He tries every alternative.

5. *The three applicants problem* (IV, 9). This is another of those puzzles that at first glance looks impossible. After all, it appears that the only thing any of the applicants can know is that at least one black mark is visible, and clearly the problem can't be solved on the basis of that piece of information alone. Therefore something else must also be known. But what? Here is where the really intelligent person, rather than feeling defeated, moves into high gear, eventually realizing that he also knows something of the reasoning process that must be going on in the applicants—and that the solution may lie in that fact. Since all three applicants raised their hands, he reasons, there were two possibilities: two black and a white or three black. If, therefore, there were a white mark on any fore-

head, two men would see one black and one white and would instantly deduce that the third mark must be black. Since this instant solution did not occur, each of the three men saw two black marks. Therefore all were black, including the mark of the successful applicant.

6. *The two cars problem* (*IV, 14*). This is a straightforward calculus problem, but one that is complicated enough to be beyond the ability of most merely amateur mathematicians. In cases like this, very bright people realize, it is usually worthwhile to look closely and see if there may be some easy shortcut to a solution. In this case, there is. The secret lies in the fact that the total time the two cars travel is one minute. Since the fly goes at 120 miles per hour (and reverses direction *immediately*), he will go two miles during that time, calculus or no calculus. The ease of the solution is enough to elicit a groan from any earnest calculus student.

7. *The chessboard problem* (*IV, 15*). Practically everyone attacks this one in precisely the wrong way —by trial and error. Using a chessboard, or perhaps just a pencil and paper, one tries repeatedly to cover the sixty-two squares with the thirty-two dominoes. No success. It is at this point, I think, that the two principal types of minds begin to diverge. The very intelligent mind, in its purposeful way, is likely to form a hypothesis—that the dominoes can't cover the squares. For if that hypothesis is correct, he is one big

step ahead of his less bright competitors. (If, of course, the hypothesis is not correct, he is off on a wild goose chase, but the alternative is simply to keep trying different ways of putting dominoes on squares.) All right, then, he asks, just *why* won't it work? He tries numbering the lines of squares; that course yields nothing worthwhile. But perhaps he does notice that a given square, if its assigned number is odd, must always combine with an even square. From there it is only a slight jump to the realization that each square has its own color and that a black square must always combine with a white. Since the two missing squares are the same color—eureka!—at the end there will always be two squares left over.

8. *The fork in the road problem* (*IV, 16*). At first it appears that there is no way, with only one question, to find out (a) if the person asked is the liar or the truth teller and (b) if his fork in the road is the right one or the wrong one. Won't the one question be used up in finding out whether the man is telling the truth or lying, leaving no way to find out the second part of the problem? Apparently so—until it occurs to the puzzler that it may somehow be possible to ask a question whose answer will not depend on which person is asked. Once he is on that trail, the idea of the double falsehood (or double truth, as the case may be) comes easily and he sees that the question to ask is: "If I were to ask you if this is the way I should go, would you say yes?" He also sees that it doesn't matter which man he asks.

9. *The multiplied letters* (*V, 1*). The peculiar beauty of this one is that it can be done in an elegantly logical way. It is worth going through step by step, as an illustration of how an apparently difficult problem yields to a certain sort of mind:

a. The puzzler realizes that, since A multiplied by 4 yields only a one-digit answer, it must be either 1 or 2.

b. Since E × 4 must yield an even number, A must be 2.

c. Since the only numbers that, when multiplied by 4, yield a figure ending with 2, are 3 and 8, E must be either 3 or 8.

d. Since A × 4 cannot be 13—*i.e.*, cannot be a two-digit number—it must be 8. Therefore E is 8.

e. Since a 3 is carried over to D in the top line, it must also be added to D in the answer. We can see that B × 4 must yield a one-digit number. That means that B must be either a 1 or a 2. If it is a 2, then with the 3 added to it, D would be 11—impossible. So B must be 1.

f. Now consider D. The question here is simple: What number, when multiplied by 4 and enlarged by the carried 3, will yield a number ending in 1? Two numbers fill the bill: 2 and 7. Since we already know that B is 1, the missing number must be 7.

g. The B in the top line must have a carried 3 added to it in order to yield 7 in the answer, so C, when its carried 3 is added to it, must be at least 30. The only numbers that will work, therefore, are 7, 8 or 9. A little experimentation shows that 9 is the missing number.

10. *The four coins puzzle (V, 13)*. A few moments' study shows that this one can't be done in two dimensions, as we assume at first it must be done. But who said it *has* to be done in two dimensions? The true puzzler, instead of trying an approach that is clearly impossible, gropes for some loophole and, with luck, quickly finds it in the third dimension. Then all he needs to do is arrange three coins in a triangle and put the fourth on top of one of them. (I will confess that this has a certain willful trickiness that many puzzlers, myself included, find distasteful. Many others, on the other hand, like puzzles that contain a certain amount of verbal trickery. *De gustibus non disputandum est.*)

These, then, are a few of the ways very nimble-witted people solve problems. Their most telling mental characteristic seems to be a restless agility that is willing to abandon an apparently fruitless approach and try another one, no matter how improbable it looks at first. (Isn't it too bad more statesmen don't think that way, too?) It can all be reduced, really, to one simple formula: *Don't give up.*

Everybody in class clear on that lesson? Final examinations follow.

VII.

So you think you're pretty bright?
(Well, maybe you are.)

In the past ten years Mensa, the high I.Q. society, has tested some 100,000 people to determine just where they rank in intelligence. To do this, the organization has developed special tests that are more challenging, more interesting, and—let's be candid about it—very often more maddeningly impenetrable than ordinary intelligence tests. The following test, modeled on those actually used by Mensa, was specially devised for this book by Mensa's research director and guru-in-residence, Max L. Fogel, Ph.D. It is, he says with an almost straight face, "not particularly tough, although some of the questions may be confusing at first." Well, don't let a little confusion discourage you; in this league, that's supposed to be part of the fun.

1. If seven belly dancers can lose a total of 20 pounds in eight hours of dancing, how many more belly dancers would be needed to lose a total of 20 pounds in only four hours of dancing provided the new dancers shed weight only half as fast as the original seven?

(a) 7   (b) 21   (c) 27   (d) 14   (e) 12

2. Some Mensa members are geniuses. All geniuses have some human virtues as redeeming qualities. Therefore:

   (*a*) Mensa members all have some virtue.
   (*b*) All geniuses are quality Mensa members.
   (*c*) Some Mensa members have redeeming qualities.

3. $\sqrt{I}$ is to C^2 as B^3 is to D times _____.
   (*a*) B   (*b*) C   (*c*) D   (*d*) E   (*e*) F

4. Fill in the blank spaces by selecting one of the four lettered alternatives.

Marlon Brando	Ingrid Bergman	Ingmar Bergman	(1)	Igor Stravinsky
Sophia Loren	(2)	Pablo Picasso	Charles Ives	Richard Burton
Luis Bunuel	Jackson Pollock	Sergei Prokofiev	(3)	(4)

   (*a*) (1) Paul Klee; (2) Rudolph Nureyev; (3) Vivien Leigh; (4) Joan Miro
   (*b*) (1) Georges Braque; (2) Federico Fellini; (3) Dustin Hoffman; (4) Elizabeth Taylor
   (*c*) (1) Jon Voigt; (2) Alfred Hitchcock; (3) Leontyne Price; (4) Richard Tucker
   (*d*) (1) Aaron Copland; (2) Paul Cezanne; (3) Helen Hayes; (4) John Wayne

5. "A stream cannot rise higher than its source" means:

(a) You decline after achieving your highest level.
(b) Streams of knowledge don't come from high sources.
(c) Your stream of consciousness is highly resourceful.
(d) Your stream of achievement is limited by your background.
(e) Gravitational factors prevent water from running uphill.

6. Which one does not belong?
   (a) dada   (b) abstract expressionist   (c) cubist
   (d) dodecaphonic   (e) pointillist

7. Consider the series of diagrams on the top line. Which diagram on the bottom line comes next in the series?

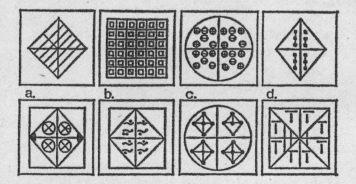

8. Which one does not belong?
   (a) chess   (b) bridge   (c) go   (d) Mah-Jongg
   (e) backgammon

9. "The used key is always bright" means:
    (a) Keep on the scene in order to stay with it.
    (b) If you use a test key you will appear bright.
    (c) New devices often don't work very well.
    (d) Old ideas are the best.

10. Complete the series: 2–4; 6–18; _____.
    (a) 8–24   (b) 8–32   (c) 10–40   (d) 20–60
    (e) 21–84

11. "A rolling stone gathers no moss" means:
    (a) None of the Rolling Stones smoke marijuana.
    (b) Shifting stones around in a rock garden prevents weeds.
    (c) Rock collections don't appreciate in value with time.
    (d) Stay in your groove to do your thing.

12. All readers of this book greatly love puzzles. Some readers of this book are famous. Some famous people are great lovers. Therefore:
    (a) All readers of this book become famous.
    (b) All great lovers are puzzling.
    (c) Some famous people love puzzles.
    (d) Some readers of this book are great lovers.

13. Greens are better farklers (farkleberry collectors, of course) than most Purples. However, in farkling competition in which the income of Greens is equal to the income of Purples, the matches are standoffs. Farkling ability has been demonstrated by independent researchers to have a possible connection with diet. The Greens have more money than the Purples and

can afford better farkling instruction. The most promising approach to equalization of farkling ability in the two groups would probably be to:

- (*a*) Provide farkling ability dietary ingredients to the Purples.
- (*b*) Equalize the wealth by giving enough Green money to Purples.
- (*c*) Make sure the Purples have sufficient nourishment for good health.
- (*d*) Obtain better farkling teachers and equipment for the Purples.

14. C, G, Q are to F, V, R as T, X, H are to:
(*a*) V, L, G   (*b*) B, F, Y   (*c*) W, M, I   (*d*) N, Z, D

15. "The good is the enemy of the best" means:
- (*a*) If you're good you'll best your enemy.
- (*b*) Be good to your best enemy.
- (*c*) Don't accept less than your best.
- (*d*) The good struggles against the best.

16. Complete the series:

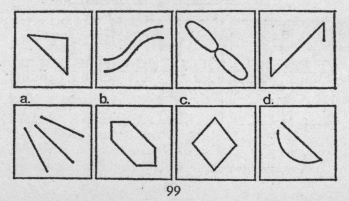

17. Grsmr kxcgob sc mybbomd?
   (a) Ylfsyecvi xyd drsc yxo.
   (b) Pybqod sd.
   (c) Iye kbo k qyyn qeoccob.
   (d) Kxydrob sxknoaekdo kddowzd.

18. Complete the series:

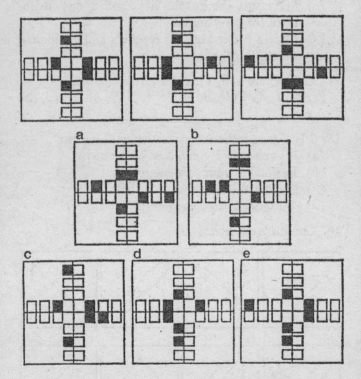

The helpers

Frederick B. Artz of Oberlin, Ohio, a man with as facile and inventive a mind as I will ever know, once observed: "You don't *cook* hash; you *accumulate* it." And so it is with this book. It is not so much a written book as an accumulated one, and it could not have been accumulated without the help of a great many selflessly brilliant people who took time to correspond with me and talk with me about puzzles that are particular favorites of theirs, as well as about questions of human intelligence in general. Among those who, for one reason or another, have earned my special thanks are:

R. C. Allais, Randolph W. Banner, Max Batchelder, Henry Bate, S. Bayne, Andrew F. Bender, Richard Boeth, Roger Brewis, Betty Burney, Jim Cochrane, Roger Crabtree, Madeline B. Cuthbertson, Crazy Eddie Epstein, H. de Grote, the late P. T. Fenn, Jr., Max L. Fogel, Michael J. H. Gerrard, I. J. Good, Bostock Hackett III, Irving Hale, E. C. Hanford, Ellis Hardy, Alice Kasman, David Greene Kolodny, Norris F. Krueger, Leo Michael Linehan, Christina M. Lyon, James MacFadyen, F. C. MacKnight, James J. Madigan, Arthur A. Merrill, Kurt Nassau, Norbert

A. Nizze, Grose Perla, John Power, Rita Schoch Sagers, Vern Schuman, Victor Serebriakoff, Samuel A. Shaffe, Easy Sloman, Joseph Smrcka, Alan E. Thompson, James F. Vance, N. A. S. Vincent, Joe Wagner, Donn Wallace, Ernest Wedge, Nelson Winget, Ethel Wollman and whoever hung the rope trick on the maple tree at the Seton Boy Scout Reservation.

Answers to puzzles

1. The next letter in the sequence O T T F F S S is E. The letters are the initial letters of *One*, *Two*, *Three*. . . . but you know the rest.

2. There are 20 9's from 1 to 100. Or did you forget 90, 91, 92, 93 . . . etc.?

3. Since the 8-inch diagonal is the same length as the circle's radius, the answer is 8 inches.

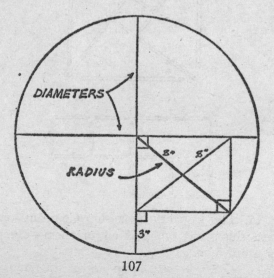

CHAPTER II

1. (a)

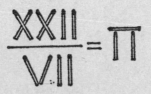

(b)

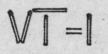

2.

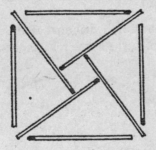

3.

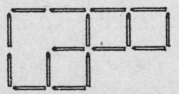

4. 15. The Equality Steamship Company operates sixteen ships and we pass all of them—except, of course, our own.

5.

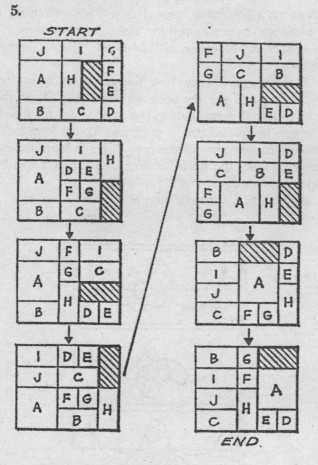

START

END.

Some intermediate steps are omitted. They can be worked out without difficulty.

6. "Squaring the circle is proclaimed impossible, but what does 'impossible' mean in mathematics? The first steam vessel to cross the Atlantic carried, as part of

its cargo, a book that 'proved' it was impossible for a steam vessel to cross anything, much less the Atlantic." —Kasner and Newman in *Mathematics and the Imagination*.

7. Although it may look impossible, it is in fact very simple to get the hook off the string. Take the loop where it passes behind the two strings on which the cup hangs and pull it until you have a loop large enough to pass around the cup. Pull the loop around the cup, from the back forward, and the cup will be released from the string.

8. Not at all. It can be done as follows:

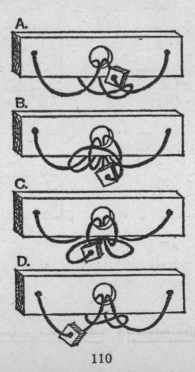

Explanation: Move the block through the loop (position A). Then pull the loop through the hole from the back to the front (position B). Pass the block from right to left through the loops as shown (position C). Pass the loop back through the hole from front to back and the block will now be on the left (position D).

10.

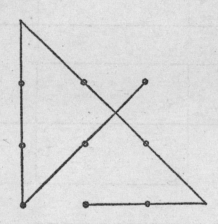

12.

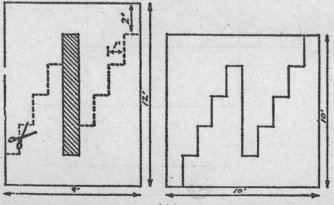

13. To visualize the problem, imagine that the room can be unfolded, like a shoebox, in various ways and that the routes of the spider to the fly can thus be

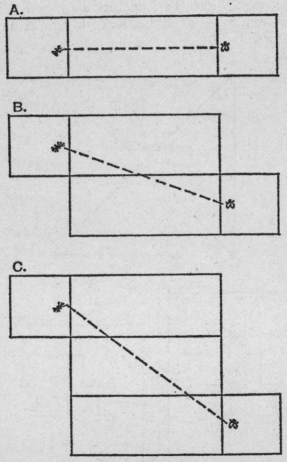

seen as if they were flat. The apparently straightest route (A) is actually the longest—42 feet. Route B requires that the spider travel slightly over 40 feet. Route C, the shortest, is exactly 40 feet.

14. Twenty-eight days. On the twenty-eighth day the snail reaches the top of the well. Once there, it does not, of course, slip backward.

15. Three hours and three minutes. Once the amoeba in the first jar has reproduced itself (a process that takes three minutes), that jar is at the same point at which the second jar started. The only difference is that it is three minutes behind.

16. Shame on you if you missed this oldie. Since the ship is afloat, the water level in relation to the ship stays the same. Therefore, eight feet are above the water at the end, just as at the beginning.

17. Pour the five-ounce container full from the jug. Pour the three-ounce container full from the five-ounce container, leaving two ounces remaining in the five-ounce container. Pour the three-ounce container back into the jug. Then pour the two ounces remaining in the five-ounce container into the three-ounce container. Pour the five-ounce container full from the jug. Fill the remaining one ounce of the three-ounce container from the five-ounce container and four ounces are left.

GAMES FOR THE SUPERINTELLIGENT

18.

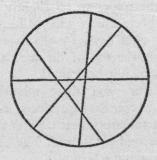

Eleven segments may be formed with the four lines. The key, of course, is that each successive line must divide as many segments as possible.

19. 160 mph. (The secret lies in converting miles per hour to miles per minute and in using fractions instead of decimals to avoid rounding errors.)

20. Assume any convenient distance for the total trip. If, for example, it is thirty miles, the first half of the trip at 15 mph requires one hour. But to average 30 mph for the total trip would require one hour. Therefore the puzzle has no solution; it is impossible.

24.

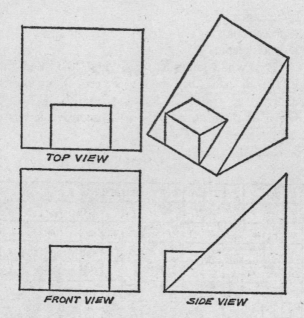

TOP VIEW

FRONT VIEW

SIDE VIEW

25. The shape is simply two intersecting cylinders, one of which has a hole bored through its center:

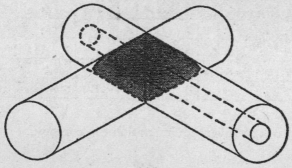

CHAPTER III

1. Strength
2. Facetious
3. Bookkeeper
4. John, while James had had "had," had had "had had." "Had had" had had a better effect on the teacher.
5. All of them contain three consecutive letters of the alphabet.
6.

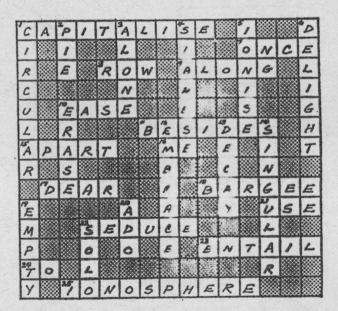

In cases of advanced frustration the composer of this

puzzle sometimes supplies hints for certain of the words as follows:

Across—1. Capital I's (British spelling)   7. One C said quickly = once   8. Greek alphabet   9. Long A = along   16. U = me, to reader   18. Bar G   22. Deuce = 2; 2 C's = seduce   23. Tail on N = entail   25. I on a sphere

Down—1. Circle R   2. Greek alphabet   3. A on its own = alone   4. E's joined at the middle = Siamese   5. I on I's   6. D as a bulb = delight   10. Raise E = erase   12. Brace of pheasants = 2 pheasants; thus embrace.   14. Single R   20. A ditto = ado   22. Sole O.

CHAPTER IV

1. White. It is a polar bear, for the North Pole is one of the places where you can go one mile south, one mile east, and one mile north, and still end up at your starting point. (The others are near the South Pole.)

2. The carpenter must use the full six cuts. To prove this, consider the middle cube. It must have six faces and each must be made with a separate cut.

3. Most people erroneously include No. 4 in their answer. But consider: No. 2 does not matter, since the question is concerned only with red cards. If No. 1 has a circle, the answer to the question is no. Similarly, if No. 3 is red the answer is no. If No. 1 is a square, No. 3 is green, and No. 4 is either red *or* green the answer is yes. Therefore the answer is: No. 1 and No. 3.

4. See Chapter 6 for the solution to this problem.

5. Weigh coins 1, 2, 3, and 4 against coins 5, 6, 7, and 8. If they balance, weigh coins 9 and 10 against coins 11 and 8 (we know from the first weighing that 8 is a good coin). If they balance, we know coin 12, the only unweighed one, is the counterfeit. The third weighing indicates whether it is heavy or light.

If, however, at the second weighing (above), coins 11 and 8 are heavier than coins 9 and 10, either 11 is heavy or 9 is light or 10 is light. Weigh 9 with 10. If they balance, 11 is heavy. If they don't balance, either 9 or 10 is light.

Now assume that at first weighing the side with coins 5, 6, 7, and 8 is heavier than the side with coins 1, 2, 3, and 4. This means that either 1, 2, 3, or 4 is light or 5, 6, 7, or 8 is heavy. Weigh 1, 2, and 5 against 3, 6, and 9. If they balance, it means that either 7 or 8 is heavy or 4 is light. By weighing 7 and 8 we obtain the answer, because if they balance then 4 has to be light. If 7 and 8 do not balance, then the heavier coin is the counterfeit.

If, when we weigh 1, 2, and 5 against 3, 6, and 9, the right side is heavier, then either 6 is heavy or 1 is light or 2 is light. By weighing 1 against 2 the solution is obtained.

If, however, when we weigh 1, 2, and 5 against 3, 6, and 9, the right side is lighter, then either 3 is light or 5 is heavy. By weighing 3 against a good coin the solution is easily arrived at.

6. The messenger is a truth teller. If the native in the distance lived on the western side of the island, and

was therefore a truth teller, he would say so. If, on the other hand, the native in the distance lived on the eastern side of the island and was therefore a liar, he would say the same thing.

7. The first man, whether or not he is an islander, did say he is white. (Either he *is* white and therefore tells the truth, or he is an islander and lies; the result is the same in either case.) The second man accurately reports what the first man said, so we know the rest of his statement is also true. Therefore he is white and the first man is white. The third man is therefore a liar and a native.

8.

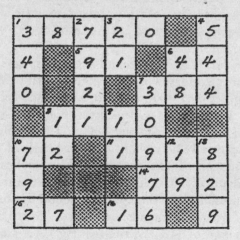

Explanation ("Across" and "Down" are indicated by "A" and "D"):

Consider 15 A. Father Dunk must walk at either 3 or 4 mph, since only these numbers yield a two-digit cube. Assume 4 mph and write 64 for 15 A.

Note 11A. The first digit must be 1, since it is a four-digit year and we have not yet reached the year 2000. Then the last digit of 16A is 3, which is also the last digit of 7D. But 7D is a square, and no square ends in 3. Therefore Father Dunk walks at 3 mph, and 15A is 27. (This yields a 6 as the last digit of 7D, possible for a square.)

Notice that 9D times 10A equals 10D. The value for 9D ends in 1 and 10D ends in 2, so that (. . 1) (?) —(. . 2). The only possible second digit for 10A is 2. By reasoning similar to that used for 11A above, we conclude that the first digit of 8A is 1. So 8D is 12. If 1⅓ the perimeter of Dog's Mead is walked in 12 minutes, then one can go around exactly once in 9 minutes; at 3 mph, that is a distance of 792 yards for the perimeter, 14A.

Consider 11A. The second digit must be an 8 or a 9; otherwise Mary would have been born before 1800, making her over 100 years old, impossible because her age in 1939, 3D, is a two-digit number. Assume the year of her birth is in the 1800s. Then it must have been at least 1839, making the third digit of 11A and the first digit of 12D at least 3. This implies that the three digits of 10D plus 1 are equal to a minimum of 39, impossible for a three-digit number. Therefore, the year of Mary's birth must be 1900 or later, making the second digit of 11A a 9, and making 7D a cube ending in 976.

Since the perimeter is 792 yards, the length plus the breadth equals 396 yards. The breadth must end in a 4 or 6 for its square (7D) to end in 6. Finally, the fact that 6D is two digits indicates that the difference between the length and breadth is less than 100 yards. Only the following dimensions satisfy these three conditions:

Length

242 240 232 230 222 220 212 210 202 200

Breadth

154 156 164 166 174 176 184 186 194 196

Only 176 yields a square ending in 976. So 7D equals 30976, and the dimensions of Dog's Mead are 220 yards by 176 yards. The value for 6A, then, is 44.

From the dimensions of Dog's Mead, it is easily calculated that the area is 32 roods, which, times 12 for 8D, yields 384 for 7A. If Ted's age (6D) is 48, Mary must be 21 for him to be twice her age in 1945. Then 3D is 21, and the year of her birth, 11A, is 1918.

Since the year the Dunks acquired Dog's Mead ends in 0 (8A), the number of years it has been in the family (13D) must end in 9, since the year is 1939. Then, 13D is 829, and 8A becomes 1110. Now 16A can be derived; it equals 16.

Recall that 9D times 10A equals 10D. And, we now see that the three digits of that product plus 1 must equal 19 (12D). Try various digits beginning with 1 for the first digit of 10A. For 1, 10A equals 12, which times 11 (9D) equals 132, whose digits plus 1 add up to 7, which is not equal to 19 (12D). By trial and error, it is found that 10A equals 72, and 10D becomes 792.

The area of Dog's Mead (1A) is 38,720 sq. yds. Note that 1D times the area of 32 roods divided by

20 shillings per pound equals the total value in pounds of Dog's Mead. Since 1D is at least 300 shillings, the value of Dog's Mead is equal to at least 480 pounds, so 4D must begin with a digit at least equal to 5 (otherwise 4D would equal 444 pounds, less than 480 pounds). Try various digits for 4D from 5 upward that will divide evenly by 32 to yield an even value (with no remainder) for 1D. Only 544 pounds works out for 4D, to give 340 for 1D.

All that remains is 2D. The only number having a four-digit square equal to 7--1 is 89, which squares to 7921. So Father Dunk's mother-in-law is 89, his Aunt Martha (5A) is 91, and the problem is done.

9. Black. See Chapter VI.

10. I. J. Good, who supplied this puzzle, explains the solution as follows: "Each person realizes that if the mark on his own forehead were white, then the puzzle for the remaining three people would be precisely the three-person puzzle. Since he knows that they are exceptionally intelligent, he knows they would be able to solve this puzzle. After a few minutes, since none of them has in fact solved it, he realizes that the mark on his own forehead must be black." Mr. Good (who is, incidentally, a University Professor in the Department of Statistics at Virginia Polytechnic Institute) adds: "The puzzle cannot be extended to five people. Even if all five are told that they are all exceptionally intelligent, there is no guarantee at any time that the others would have been able to solve the four-person puzzle."

11. Gloria loves Arthur.

12. There are 10 birds and 20 animals. The problem may be expressed in equation form as follows, letting A represent animals and B represent birds:

$$A + B = 30$$
$$4A + 2B = 100$$

13. Harry is the pitcher, Allen the catcher, Paul the first baseman, Jerry the second baseman, Andy the third baseman, Ed the shortstop, Sam the left fielder, Mike the right fielder, and Bill the center fielder.

14. The fly traveled two miles. See Chapter VI.

15. It can't be done. See Chapter VI.

16. He asks either man, "If I were to ask you if this is the way I should go, would you say yes?" If the man he asks is the one who tells the truth, he will of course get the right answer. If the man he asks is the man who always lies, that man lies about the answer he would give, thus giving the correct answer. By forcing the liar to lie twice, one lie negating the other, the man forces him to tell the truth.

17. Three.

CHAPTER V

1. See Chapter VI.
2. 9567
   +1085
   ─────
   10652
3. The extra square results from the slight inaccuracy of the drawing of just one line, or from the

mental assumption that the hypotenuses of the two smaller triangles are in an exact straight line. The discrepancy amounts to about 3 per cent of the large triangle's area.

4. All of the numbers are the number 16, written in different bases. The first is written in the base 16, the second in the base 15, etc., down to the last, which is written in the base 1. The missing number, therefore, is 121.

5. (c)

6. 50 minutes.

7. 1 lb., 3 lbs., 9 lbs., and 27 lbs. In most cases, of course, various combinations of weights must be put on both sides of the scale.

8. 17 men, 13 women, 90 children.

9. 5 ¾ inches long.

10. 40 mph.

11. About 5 ¾ inches.

12. (a) The rudimentary formula that brought an end to inexact tallying of possessions or exchange.

(b) Sir Isaac Newton's formula for gravitation.

(c) Einstein's formula for the conversion of matter to energy.

(d) John Napier's logarithm formula, which provided a multiplication and division method simply by adding or subtracting the logarithms of numbers.

(e) Pythagoras' formula for the relationship of the two sides and hypotenuse of a right triangle.

(f) Ludwig Boltzmann's equation for the behavior of gases.

(g) Konstantin Tsiolkovskii's equation giving

the changing speed of a rocket as it burns the weight of its fuel.

(h) Louis de Broglie's equation for light as a form of energy.

(i) James Clerk Maxwell's formula equating electricity and magnetism.

(j) Archimedes' formula for the lever.

13. See Chapter VI.

CHAPTER VII

1. d
2. c
3. e
4. b
5. d
6. d
7. b
8. b
9. a
10. e
11. d
12. c
13. a
14. c
15. c
16. b
17. c
18. a

By the year 2000, 2 out of 3 Americans could be illiterate.

It's true.

Today, 75 million adults… about one American in three, can't read adequately. And by the year 2000, U.S. News & World Report envisions an America with a literacy rate of only 30%.

Before that America comes to be, you can stop it… by joining the fight against illiteracy today.

Call the Coalition for Literacy at toll-free **1-800-228-8813** and volunteer.

Volunteer Against Illiteracy. The only degree you need is a degree of caring.

Ad Council · Coalition for Literacy

Warner Books is proud to be an active supporter of the Coalition for Literacy.